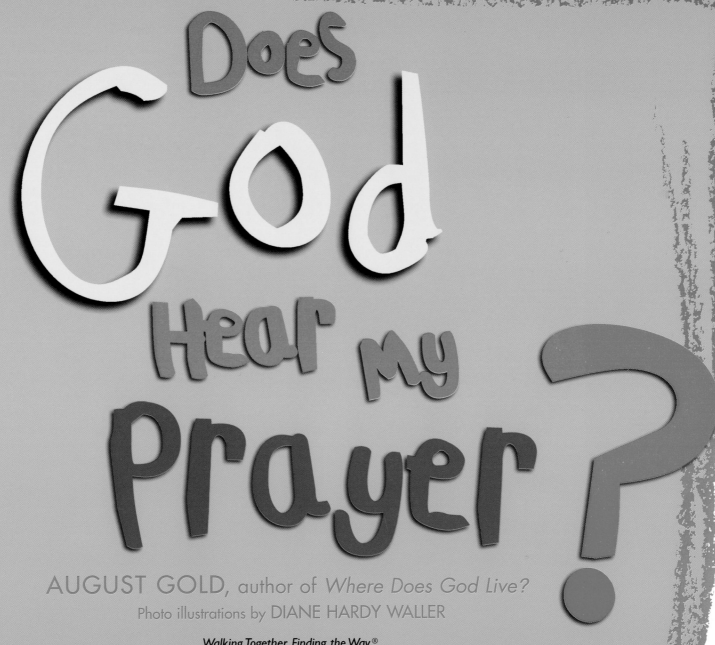

Does God Hear My Prayer?

AUGUST GOLD, author of *Where Does God Live?*

Photo illustrations by DIANE HARDY WALLER

Walking Together, Finding the Way®

SKYLIGHT PATHS®
PUBLISHING

Woodstock, Vermont

It was a shiny red bike
you saw in the store—

"God, give me this bike and I won't ask for more!"

Under the covers
you prayed through the night,
but when morning came
there was no bike in sight.

Mom and Dad came running
at your angry cry.

"God didn't hear me!
Mom, tell me **why!**"

Dad hugged you and said,

"God hears you—

it's true,

but praying doesn't mean
God takes orders from you!"

"But if I don't pray
to get my own way,
then how do I talk to God?
Mom, what should I say?"

"Bring God your friendship,
        your **questions** and **fears,**
bring God your laughter
                and also your **tears."**

"Do I use a prayer from a book or make one up in my head?"

"God welcomes all prayers,"
Mom wisely said.

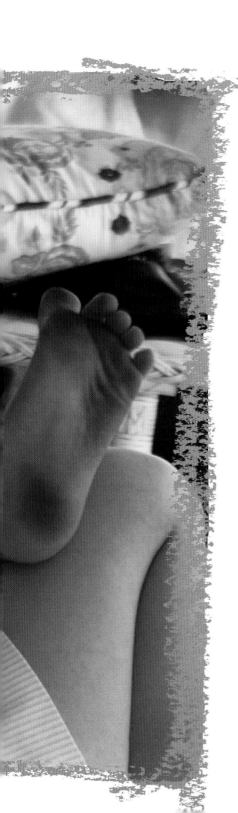

"God always listens
to your thoughts and words;
even your feelings
are felt and are heard."

"But when I stop
talking to God about me,
what does God do then?
Does God just agree?"

"When you are all done
praying from your heart,

that's when it's time
for your listening to start.

"Ssshhh and get quiet
and let your thoughts fade away,

so you hear the whisperings
of what God has to say ...

"To all that you bring God,
God returns only love;
you're forever together
like a hand in a glove.

"You are God's treasure
and will always be.

God loves us as we are—
we are *all* God's family.

"God helps us remember
     that God lives in the world,

through the wide open hearts
of every boy and girl.

"So prayer isn't telling

God what to do—

it is letting God help you

remember what's true."

Oh, this makes you happy
and feel a lot less alone,
knowing that in your heart
God is at home.

You now know God listens
and holds you dear,

and all the help you need
will always be near.

Now God seems friendly
and praying, fun—
so your friendship with God
has already begun!

Does God Hear My Prayer?

Second Printing 2011
Text © 2005 by August Gold
Photos © 2005 by Diane Hardy Waller

Library of Congress Cataloging-in-Publication Data
Gold, August, date.
Does God hear my prayer? / August Gold ; photographs by Diane Hardy Waller.
p. cm.
ISBN-10: 1-59473-102-0 (pbk.)
ISBN-13: 978-1-59473-102-0 (pbk.)
1. Prayer—Juvenile literature. I. Waller, Diane Hardy. II. Title.
BV212.G59 2005

2004019161

10 9 8 7 6 5 4 3 2
Manufactured in China

Interior design concept: Michael Ingersoll and Greg Zukowski
Cover design & interior typesetting: Jenny Buono
Special thanks to City Bicycles (www.citybicyclesny.com) for their kind assistance with the photograph appearing on page 2. The photograph on page 27 is copyright of Gisele Wright, reprinted courtesy of iStockphoto.com; photo page 31 copyright by Carol Logen.

SkyLight Paths Publishing is creating a place where people of different spiritual traditions come together for challenge and inspiration, a place where we can help each other understand the mystery that lies at the heart of our existence.

SkyLight Paths sees both believers and seekers as a community that increasingly transcends traditional boundaries of religion and denomination—people wanting to learn from each other, *walking together, finding the way*®.

SkyLight Paths, "Walking Together, Finding the Way" and colophon are trademarks of LongHill Partners, Inc., registered in the U.S. Patent and Trademark Office.

Walking Together, Finding the Way®
Published by SkyLight Paths Publishing
A Division of LongHill Partners, Inc.
Sunset Farm Offices, Route 4, P.O. Box 237
Woodstock, Vermont 05091
Tel: (802) 457-4000   Fax: (802) 457-4004
www.skylightpaths.com